MW01045098

"WORDS"

JOYCE MARTIN

With Love;

Joyce Martin

xulon PRESS

Copyright © 2015 by Joyce Martin

"Words"
by Joyce Martin

Printed in the United States of America.

ISBN 9781498456111

All rights reserved solely by the author. The author guarantees all contents are original and do not infringe upon the legal rights of any other person or work. No part of this book may be reproduced in any form without the permission of the author. The views expressed in this book are not necessarily those of the publisher.

Scripture quotations taken from the The Living Bible (TLB). Copyright © 1971 by Tyndale House. Used by permission.

Scripture quotations taken from the American Standard Version (ASV)- public domain

www.xulonpress.com

Table of Contents

"WORDS"

Words that fall upon our ears
Can deem all things changed.
It all depends in what order
Those words have been arranged.

Loneliness can be healed and
New friendships can start.
Love can be shown verbally
As feelings from the heart.

Songs are sung from lyrics that
Were once only a word.
God gives us free range on the
Message we want heard.

"The Walk Of Life"

Come my friend and walk this life with me
Let's talk, sing, and frolic by the sea.

Barefoot, with warm sand between our toes.
We will reveal secrets and share our woes.

Come my friend and walk this life with me.
Let's linger by the fireside sipping tea,

Sit by a brook and watch the calming flow.
Plant seeds of kindness to watch them grow.

Come walk with me, my dear friend of old,
Lets' dwell in past memories of gold.

Then to avoid the shadows of aging in sight,
We will walk hand in hand, facing the light.

"RECIPE FOR HAPPINESS "

Take all of your fond memories, blend with what
You've learned from peers.
Toss in a little humor, trust in God
And add a cup of tears.

Stir in self-esteem and confidence. Then throw
Out all your fears.
Blend this all together in a warm and loving heart
And simmer it in cheers.

When well done, you'll have contentment,
To last you through your years.

"THE LONG MILE"

As a child I lived on a farm
- About a mile from the hard top road
This mile was good in fair weather,
But the dickens when it rained or snowed.

There seemed to be no bottom
To this soil of rich red clay.
We often had to use horses
To pull our car part way.

Once over this mile it was smooth sailing.
To our planned destination.
Though the deep tracks that remained,
Were to me an inspiration.

Because long after the weather cleared
And the road grader came,
There would always be a next time,
The difficulty the same.

Of all the places it took us
By forging this long miserable mile,
On looking back upon it,
Like life, it must have been worthwhile.

"CHURCH IN THE SMOKIE'S"

Deep in the Smokie's sit's a little white church.
It's a beauty in itself just to view.
Its bountiful blessings are worth the search.
But the roads that take you there are few.

There are Churches like this all over God's land.
Their chiming bells too, ring loud and clear.
Some are on a beautiful mountainside,
          some on sand.
They are all calling you, God's message to hear.

View the scenery, travel the winding trail.
Listen to the silence calling out your name.
Hear the pealing bells throughout the vale.
Find what you're missing, learn of "God's fame."

A visit to this chapel can turn your life around.
It's bells ring clear and if you answer the call.
Life's most precious treasures can be found.
Through God there is peace and salvation for all.

"A LOOK AT LIFE"

A look at life from where you stand
May seem confusing and out of hand.
Untruth and distrust have spread o'er this land.
All are out of control like a fire that's fanned.

Faith has been placed in the wrong hands,
These are not our Saviors plans.
Look to Christ, see how He stands,
Strong and sure with outstretched hands.

Let's join together and form a band,
Put truth and trust back on the stand.
Let "God "control as He has planned,
And fan "His" fame as He commands.

"THE HIGHWAYS OF YOUR MIND"

Through the highways of your mind,
Yield your heart unto the Lord.
Through crowded traffic as you wind,
Cruise this life with true accord.

Watch for speed zones, be alert.
Keep your self-control intact,
It could be others that you hurt
If you leave a bad impact.

Through the highways of your mind
Think thoughts pure and true.
Be aware of what's behind.
But keep this present life in view.

Take a side road for a change,
Leave your troubles all behind.
Let God keep you in free range.
To all His children, do be kind.

Be prepared to make quick turns
If God guides you with a sign.
Proceed with caution and concern,
Through the Highways of your mind.

"GROWING LOVE "

We all have our own little world
In which we live our lives.
Our actions are the seeds of our future'
We only reap what thrives.

While toiling this earth for instant joy.
And seeking life's greatest pleasures,
We plant our world with undo stress,
Sometimes ignoring true treasures.

We often have to weed our world
Of thrones, power, tare and greed.
Throw out bitterness, jealousy and hate
That's in the life we lead.

Then through God we can truly find
The pleasures that we seek
And sow loving seeds of kindness
For friends and loved ones to reap.

"ACTIVE LOVE"

March   to the beat of the love in your heart.

Cling   to your faith and let the
healing start.

Dig   out resentments that lay heavy on
your soul.

Resolve   all anger, don't let tempers
take control

Climb   the ladder of forgiveness from
bottom to top.

Teach   this virtue to others, until their
angers stop.

Move   your faith to higher grounds of
giving love.

Pray   non -ceasing to your Father
up above.

Open   paths that once you feared to trod.

Search   for good in all, they too were
made by God.

Fight   the battle when obstacles block
your way.

Give   them to the Lord and go about your day.

Jump   into the waters and flood the church's needs.

Reach   out to your brother, be the one who leads.

Run   the Christian race, leave your footprints on His land'

Love   is not an option, it is our LORD'S COMMAND!

"COME FLY WITH JESUS"

Get on board with Jesus,
Bring your friends!
Everyone is Welcome
As this flight ascends.
Leave that excess baggage
At the gate.
There will be no room for anger
Or for hate.
"God" will be our pilot
Day and night.
We'll soar above dissention
On this flight.
We will fly in rumbling weather
With no fears.
And if life's ride gets bumpy
"He" will dry our tears.
When Life's flight is over,
Be not alas.
"God" will fly us all to heaven'
All First Class!

"READ THE SCRIPT'

You turned this page
To read the script.
Perhaps you're searching
For pleasure, maybe a lift.

Are you looking for joy or
Peace of mind?
Hoping your troubled thoughts
To leave behind?

Stop and think of the days
Just gone by.
Did they drag or did they
Seem to fly?

Were the people in your day treated
Kind and fair?
Remember your loved ones did you
Tell them you care?

You think "they already know this".
Of course they do.
But they need reassurance, which will
Also strengthen you.

"THE DRIVE"

SHOP, SHOP, SHOP
Those bargain isles!
FIND, FIND, FIND.
Your proper size.
READ, READ, READ
The labels twice.
SAVE, SAVE, SAVE.
You are so wise.
BUY, BUY, BUY.
They're all half price!
BRING, BRING, BRING.
Them home with you.
HANG, HANG, HANG,
Them on your rack.
GAIN, GAIN, GAIN.
An inch or two.
PACK, PACK, PACK.
Them in a sack.
GIVE, GIVE, GIVE.
Them to the "Drive"
SAME, SAME, SAME.
Old thing next fall.
HOW, HOW, ELSE
Would the Drive survive?
THANKS, THANKS!
GOES TO THE MALL

"MAJOR PROBLEMS IN LIFE"

Major problems usually
Stem from;

Messages not heard;
Stories not told;
Love not shown;
Words not spoken;
Marriages failed;
Communications blurred.

The Solution;
Nip them in the bud;

Listen carefully;
Tell your story;
Show your love;
Voice your opinion;
Covet your marriage;
Clarify your desires.

"THE MARCH FOR CHRIST"

As Christians we are sent out in life to do
Gods work.
We will meet Christians and those looking for
Christ for the first time.

Those searching may not know exactly what
they are looking for.
They feel disconnected and lack peace of mind.

We were put here to find these searching souls,
To Love them and help guide their spirits.

To help them find contentment that can
only be achieved,
By finding and knowing Christ as their
personal Savior.

Then they will be sent out to do the same
for others.
"The March For Christ "goes on and on, forever.

"TO MY CHILDREN"

You may not be world famous
Or a talented movie star.
But the life you have lived
Has made you who you are.

You may not be a Picasso,
Brahms or Hemmingway.
But all of you are special
In your individual way.

Your early years were shared,
Though you really had no choice.
The future is what you make it.
Speak a proud and loving voice.

Give thanks to God for memories
And the good times you have had.
Then thank Him twice and twice again
For helping through the bad.

"YOU DON'T SAY."

We can't always express ourselves
With what we want to say.
We must sometimes bite our tongue
And look the other way.

How rude it would be if we said,
"My, you're getting fat.
Or, "You sure look silly
In your new red hat."

And never, never say, "You look bad,
Have you been ill.?"
You just can't say some things
But you can bet,

YOUR CHILDREN WILL!

"BUILDING"

I'm building something for my children,
I work on it every day.
They don't know what's being done
As they go their merry way.

Pieces I will put in place,
Right before their eyes.
They help me with this project,
Though they don't realize.

Sometimes they suggest things
That's exactly what I need.
A thought, an occasion, a dream
Can be a planted seed.

We are lacking in wealth, even health,
And have quite common ways.
But you see, I'm building "Fond memories"
Into each of their childhood days.

"KENNEY"

My son I prayed for down on bended knee.
"Please guide him Lord, his way he cannot see.
The proper way to guide him
it seems I haven't found."
Before next eve they told me,
"Your son has drowned."

Was this the way God answered
can I ever pray again?
What do I do now when my children are in sin?
This took time and patience for me
to see the light.
My son was saved, he had actually won his fight.

He belonged to God first,
he was just mine on loan.
A special baby boy for me to love
and call my own.
Memories of his youth will always be a delight.
And I thank the Lord for Kenney,
every day and night.

"THE PILL"

The dumbest thing I've ever done,
At least it feels that way to me,
Was trying to nurture Jim, my teenage son,
When in football he badly hurt his knee.

After surgery and all that sordid stuff,
The Doctor said, as he sent us home,
"Here is ONE pain pill, in case it gets rough."
So in the night I heard him toss and groan.

He was upstairs, all alone and in pain!
He needed love, attention and his "pill."
So comfort he could obtain.
So; at three AM I had the goods to fill,

Ready to take to him in bed.
And,
"Yes,"
"I took the pill instead!"
Sorry; Jim.

"WHERE ARE MY CHILDREN?"

"My Children! Where are they?"
I have searched the back yard and under
the rugs.
There were five underfoot just yesterday.
I miss their antics and yearn for their hugs.
I'll search some more upstairs
And under the tables.
Maybe they are on the roof again,
Hiding in the gables.

"They are grown" someone told me.
What are they saying?
They were here just a few days ago.
All were playing.
Could time possibly
Have passed this quick?
Or is some cruel prankster
Playing a trick?

Well they were mine while It did last.
I just didn't know that time could
Go so fast."

"COLLEGE BREAK"

My beautiful daughter came home on break
To design her wedding dress, then make.
She worked diligently with
confidence and poise.
It felt good to be away from the "Dorm" noise.

She carefully added yards of ribbon and lace.
Just her and her Mom,
alone at Mom's place.
It was now time to try on her fine "Piece of Art."
So she stripped to her undies with
a pounding heart.

Suddenly someone entered
the front door unannounced.
What was that?!!! She said as she pounced.
In a panic she hid behind the patio drape.
"Whew," she said, "That was a narrow escape."

Turning around she realized she was on display,
To a group of boys with a ballgame in play.

PS; 'I'm still laughing,
With Love, Mom

"CHILD # FIVE"

Then there was Brenda, Child number FIVE.
She kept the entire world alive.

The name "Brenda!" was spoken loud and plain'
Mostly in "love" but sometimes in vain.

Her humor and love was trying and loving to all.
Also entertaining, and never, never, dull.

When she was five we moved across town.
With sidewalks, flowerbeds, and trees all around.

A perplexing day, was when she picked the
flowers next door!
Then SOLD them to "their" next door neighbor.

We were just lucky it didn't start a
neighborhood war.

However, her loving soul has given me
fond memories galore
And beautiful loving grandchildren of four.
What mother could ask for anything more?
I love you Brenda!
By; Your Mother;

"TO MY SISTER "

To my sister who's been like a mother to me.
We have literally been through thick and thin.
It hasn't been easy, we both agree.
But the rewards have been a million times ten.

She was the oldest of four
and always had her say,
But I was the youngest and usually got my way.

My sister has been a loving friend, so true.
We've shared recipes, dishes, books and tears.
We've shopped, played, worked
and yes, schemed too.
She's cried with me through my
troubles and fears.

She always laughs at all of my children's pranks.
For all of this I truly say "thanks."

One of us will surely go first, leaving the
other behind.
We served our Savoir well and know we'll
meet again.
Though saddened, the other must keep in mind
This time it will be forever and without stress
or pain.
We'll pick up on our friendship and never
be alone
Only one thing worries me, "Does Heaven
have a phone?"

"TO MY DEAR FRIEND MARY JANE"

We were very young when we first met.
We neither remember the special event.
I remember that your mother was very kind.
And your sister had beauty undefined.

Your mother baby sat me from time to time.
You helped her by keeping me in line.
After all you was the leader, you see,
Because you were five months older than me.

You taught me to play without fear.
We traveled by grinder, far and near.
I peddled very hard, you was the guide.
We traveled the world, side by side.

We played house, farmer and church.
We sang, preached and played hide
and search.
My family moved to a farm far away.
They took me along, I had no say.

However I took those fond memories along.
They helped very much when things went wrong.
As always, time swiftly moved on.
You became a nurse, I became a Mom.

Time has passed now, "Old Age" has set in,
However, we live close together again.

continued on next page

Our memories and families we can still share.
Yes, we are once again a "pair."

PS; One day at the mall a kind lady said:
"How cute"
We neither knew what to do or say, so we
put our walkers in high gear and sped away.

"TEACH ME TO PRAY"

This note was found neatly folded and placed
inside a Sunday School Teacher's bible.
Dear Teacher;
Would you hold my hand and teach
me to pray?
I try but the proper words just
won't come my way.
The Bible says that Jesus held
children by the hand.
He taught them to pray and led them
ore His land.
If I prayed to Jesus I know He
would be my friend.
Then I could walk beside Him,
no rule would I bend.
Jesus could hold my hand and
guide me all my life!
I could have peace and love,
there would be no strife.
If I just knew what to say.
PS; Would you be my friend?

The teacher prayed about this, asking the Lord to
guide her so she would know the proper words
to say when replying to this letter. Suddenly she
realized she was doing exactly what her student
was doing, hunting for the proper words. Her
reply was posted in plain sight.

continued on next page

Dear Students;
I would love to be your friend, pray and hold your hand,
But there is something You, Me and Others need to understand.
God through Jesus knows our hearts, thoughts and all that we plan.
All He ask of us is to love, worship and obey His command.
He will hear your prayer clearly, though commonly spoke.
You see; God knows all languages, even from us common folk.
Next Sunday morning as the teacher stood before her class it was clear
That the face behind that big smile was the one who struggled with "what to say."
She spoke saying;
"Class; let's stand in a circle and hold each other's hand.
Let's let the Lord know who we are and where we stand.
Let's smile and let our friends know that Jesus loves them too.
He will hear our prayers from, EVERY RACE AND EVERY HUE."

"TODAY IS TODAY"

Today is today,
Yesterday is gone,
Tomorrow is what we make it.
Because of the decisions and choices
We made along life's way,
We are who we are today

We can't change the past
It's ours to keep forever.
We can learn from it however.
With regrets amended,
Our futures can indeed be changed
If choices are rearranged.

We can separate ourselves
From the life we want to leave.
And a new life we can weave.
Then when peace has come
And all fears are gone,
Thank the Lord and pass it on!

"STEP BY STEP"

As a child, there was a dark stairway
That led to mysterious rooms above.
It was frightening and mysterious
Because to me it's destiny was unknown.
Exploring those rooms as years went by,
I found them friendly and filled with love.

Life is like that dark stairway.
With fears of pain and being alone.
STEP BY STEP we should eagerly clime
Those stairs to a higher level of life.
A life with the Lord as our master
And past memories as lessons of gold.

We must hang onto those learned lessons,
To help with our troubles in life.
The Lord will take our hand and guide us
Allowing happiness and love to unfold.
Thank Him for all the good times you had,
Then thank Him twice and twice again
For helping through the bad.

"RECIPET FOR HAPPINESS "

Take all of your fond memories, blend with what
You've learned from peers.

Toss in a little humor, trust in God
And add a cup of tears.

Stir in self-esteem and confidence.
Then throw out all your fears.

Blend this together in a warm and loving heart
And simmer it in cheers.

When well done, you'll have contentment,
To last you through your years.

"MY MOTHER'S COOKBOOK"

My mother's cookbook gave such joy through
the years.
It's easy to pick her favorites by the icing smears.

As we turn page by page, and find
the corners bent,
It will often remind us of a very special event.

Here is one for Chocolate Éclairs and Cream
Puffs Supreme.
She always took these to Aunt Nora's piled
high with cream.

And Plumb pudding, what great times that
does recall.
When all of our cousins came for Thanksgiving
each fall.

Oh look, here's Dad's recipe for homemade gin.
Remember the winter the big snow storm
came in?

Mom used all of her reserve "emergency stock".
We sat by the fireside, sang hymns and had a
good talk.

How could a cook book bring such joys?
We all like to remember when we were girls
and boys.

"SATURDAY NIGNT"

"Yep "it's Saturday night.

And you know what that means.
Mom thinks the entire world "CLEANS"!

Rub a dub, dub, out come the tubs

Some folks have a round and oblong too.
Nothing fancy for us, Old Square will do.

One kettle of water that's very hot
And a pale of cold, filled to the top.

Makes that bath water just right.

"Yep" it's Saturday night!

"GRANDMA ON THE GO"

My Grandmother, who was 4 Ft. 10 In.
Was widowed at a very young age.
Back in those days it was hard
For a woman alone.
So she sold her home, packed her trunk
And hit the road.
When illness hit she was there,
Johnnie on the spot.
If there was a garden to hoe or peas to can,
That was her next stop.
Babysitting, she loved that, and quilting,
Whatever the need may be.
She would bring her trunk
With bible on the top and dig right in.
She made braided rugs
From the worn fabric bag.
She made doll quilts and sugar cookies.
Then she was off to the next family in need.
The love she left behind each visit will always
Remain as one of my fondest memories.
"My Grandma On The Go!"

"BIRDS IN THE SNOW"

Taws' nearing Christmas and a huge amount of
snow fell.
We were to have our yearly Church program
and all about Jesus tell.
Dad was reluctant to go and was very set in
his way.
He felt, "What the need of this Christ Child to
guide us each day?

So when the special night of the program finally
rolled around,
Dad said, Ill not get out with all this snow on
the ground.
So Mom wrapped us all up warm and away
we went.
We were excited about the beautiful snow and
the special event.

Dad sat by the fireside in his favorite chair,
content as could be,
When suddenly a strange noise from outside
drew his curiosity to see.
There was a flock of distressed birds hunting
shelter from the snow.
"I'll open the barn door," He thought.
"These birds will freeze, I know."

He put his coat and boots on, hurrying as fast
as he could,

continued on next page

To open the barn door wide so the birds would
have shelter and food.
However the birds in fright flew here and there,
ignoring the good deed.
That Dad was offering them of life, warmth, and
food of seed.

He tried to drive them, shoo them, and even
turned on a light.
So the freezing birds could get warm but they
continued in flight.
This bothered Dad very much for he was a
good kind man.

He desperately thought, "I am trying hard and
doing all I can."
Suddenly it crossed his mind, "If I could only be
a bird and talk,
Then I could fly inside the barn and be followed
by the flock."

This brought Dad to his knees in prayer, he
truly understood,

Why God sent His Son to show us the way and
save all He could.
Dad had been shown through this flight of birds
why we need the Lord.
When we returned Dad was still kneeling there
as joyful tears flowed.

"GOING BACK"

Finally you've gotten where you really
want to be.
Now those fondest dreams you can actu-
ally see.
Long hard hours have earned you a nice
retirement.
It's hard to realize how fast all those
years went.
Your dream has come true! Now. You'll hurry
and pack.
You can pull up roots because you're finally
going back!
Yes back to your hometown where all of your
friends will be.
The list is all make out of whom and what you
want to see.

First of course, to ride with Mr. Smith on the
rural mail route.
Then to the corner drug store where all the
gang hung out.
And to the fishing pond where many hours
were spent
Spinning tales with Uncle Ned. My, he was
such a" Gent".
Then a nice long walk through those
peaceful woods.
Those tall pines have helped nurture all sorts
of moods.

So off you go, a bit rough now, but down the
old highway.
There's the corner drug! Good grief! It's now a
big café!

Such busy people hurrying to and from lunch.
It's depressing to think a place could change
so much.
The names on the mailboxes are not at all
the same.
With the Industrial plant and smog, a new gen-
eration came.
The fishing pond is polluted now and Uncle
Ned is at rest.
A fire left those beautiful pines, scrubs at best.
Before you go, talk to others who have walked
this path you walk.
How quickly about their true feelings they will
talk.

Observe the enthusiasm they seem to lack
Each one will tell you, "You really can't "GO
BACK."

"THE ANTHUM OF SPRING"

Spring steps in like a marching band,
With all its beauty at the weather's command.
Robins chirp as they build their nest,
While flowers spring up with musical zest.

Trees bud as directed by nature's hand,
While seeds pop up through sun warmed sand.
Rhythm builds to a climatic high,
As lightning bolts across the sky.

Then the wind softens as light breezes chime
And raindrops fall in four- four time.
It's time now for creation's note
To give the earth its colorful coat.

The first rose does a solo at the judge's stand,
With a standing ovation and a welcoming hand.
Warm sun rays shine and birds sing.
As nature performs
"The Anthem Of Spring."

"JUNE"

Here comes June, she's such a flirt,
With her low hung moon and flowers on her skirt.

She puts love in our hearts from her
magic potions.
It makes us plan weddings and parties with
loving emotions.

Of course, June, with such dignity,
is the featured guest.
She shares her beauty with all, with such
musical zest.

Corsages and bouquets need her special touch.
Everyone loves June, she gives so much.

Then June is gone, but her effects live on and on
Through –June- July,–August, and on and on.

"Follies Of Fall"

Rehearsals have started for the
upcoming show.
The Star is "Foliage", so colorfully aglow.
Her exquisite beauty will usher in" fall."
Delightfully gracious and breathtaking to all.

The stage is all set now and ready for view.
Those playing a roll all wait for their cue.
Thunder gives the drum roll for this
grand parade,
Then lightning flashes to signal,
all plans are made.

The curtain goes up! The show has begun!
All preparations for the show are done.
Bears exhibit their new fur coats,
While the owl fine tunes his hooting notes.

Geese get in line for their scheduled flight.
It's all such a spectacular, fabulous sight.
Leaves fall in their aerobic way,
Then end the show with a fabulous plie!

"SHADOWS"

Upon each life
A few shadows will fall.
It's not just you
It happens to all.

Things don't always happen
Just like they were planned.
Sometimes it seems
Like we are treading sand.

However no battle is ever won
Without a fight.
So to avoid life's shadows,
Walk facing God's Light.

"YOU"

Oh what different ways we find
To tell what's on our troubled mind.

Anxiety comes out in forms of fear,
Frustration, when needing someone near.

Anger tells a story too,
It comes out in ways untrue.

Not always feeling good and kind
Makes ones true self hard to find.

First must come the will to know
Our real emotions, not what we show.

Why you feel the way we do.
Is what you gain by knowing YOU.

"VISION"

Send me a VISION, show me a scheme.
"How To Live Peaceful" could be the theme.

Extend me a hand, show me you care.
Show me some love, which would be rare.

Give me soft clouds to soften the blows.
And a tender smile would really ease my woes.

Pease of mind would be perfectly dear.
And a summer breeze to dry my tear.

Silence of the valleys would sooth my ears
Beautiful mountains would calm my fears.

Just teach me how to be content
Then send me out to join life's "Great Event."

God's theme would serve me quite well.
With this plan I'll be sure to excel.

"COMFORT"

Surround me in comfort, wrap me in arms
of love.
Let me hear violins play soft music from above.

This should make you happy but there is one
forgotten thing.
What we receive doesn't bring joy.
Its giving that makes hearts sing.

Comfort those in sorrow, surround your friends
with love.
Speak gently to all, it will sound like it came
from "Heaven 'above."

Be kind to the less fortunate and wipe away
their tears.
Teach them how prayer will comfort pain and
conquer fears.

This will make them happy, no exception to
the rule.
And you'll reap a harvest of comfort, and feel
like a jewel.

"A BLESSING IN DISGUISE"

Some were nurtured by those who had a
faith in God.
Others struggled in life and were left
alone to trod.

Those struggles may have been a blessing
in disguise.
You may have strength you wouldn't have
otherwise.

Don't blame others, we have all been vandaled
We will be judged by how the events were
handled.

Those woes may have been a planted seed,
Planted by our Savior, to see if
we take heed.

What seems like barriers may be a bridge,
in fact,
To help us over troubles and keep our souls intact.

We can separate ourselves from what we want
to leave.
With God's help, a new life we can weave.

When peace has come and all fears are gone,
"Thank the Lord "and pass it on.

"A MESSAGE OF HOPE"

When darkness falls upon our lives,
And there seems to be no end,
Remember, pity is what thrives,
Hindering our broken hearts to mend.

Turn toward the light, though dim,
And the Lord will lighten your way,
If you only believe in Him.
He can turn your night into day.

You then have His almighty help
To guide you through your days.
His "Help" is a message of Hope
And Hope helps us in so many ways.

"MAJOR PROBLEMS"

MAJOR PROBLEMS in life
Stem from;

MESSAGES not heard;
STORIES not told;
LOVE not shown;
WORDS not spoken;
MARRIGES failed;
AND
COMMUNICATIONS blurred.

THE SOLUTIONS;

NIP them in the bud;
LISTEN carefully;
TELL your story;
SHOW your love;
VOICE your opinion;
COVET your marriage;
CLEARIFY your desires.

"MY PILLAR OF STRENGTH"

Many friends have said; "You should
write a book."
The first thought that ran through my mind was:
" Who would believe it if I did? "

However; if the message could be conveyed
that there
Can be content and peace in the middle
of chaos
Then it would be worth writing about.
"My life that is."

A strong Christian Faith has been:
"My Pillar Of Strength".
And it can be yours too, from God, just for the
asking.

That does not keep bad things from
occurring. It does
However, help the healing of your mind,
heart and soul
When bad things happen to you.

"PEOPLE AND TIME"

People and time are what is needed
When a soul is down and feels defeated.

Seek out someone with a broken heart,
Give them some time, help give them a start.

To achieving a small but important goal
Of living each day, just playing a role.

Of being a person in their troubled world
When into sorrow their life has been hurled.

This will be rewarding, and needless to say,
It may be YOU needing "PEOPLE AND TIME"
Someday.

"THE ROAD OF LIFE"

The "Road of Life", when viewed
From now,
Presents a challenge and questions
Of "how"?
With so many decisions there are
To make,
How can one possibly know which path
To take?

The "Joys Of Life" 'when viewed
Looking back
Have been the challenges we
Dared attack.
The decisions made whether right
Or wrong,
Are the memories cherished
As we travel along.

"THE STORMS OF CHANGE"

The Storms of change blow fierce
Our aching hearts and souls they pierce.

Dreams are shattered by the wind,
Making our stressed life slow to mend.

Stress comes in with much a due
Perhaps a change is overdue.

Quite often we just don't understand.
Recall, its God who is in command.

Within your heart, do make alms.
Only then the storm flurry calms.

"LEARN FROM YOUE HEARTACHES"

Take the heartaches of your past
And use wisely what you've learned.
Be sure anger has been cast.
Then show others you're concerned.

Teach them how the Lord can heal.
Tell them what He's done for you.
Pray with others as you kneel
And help their spirit to renew.

Let them know of what you gain
When the "Lord "is by your side.
As you suffer loss and pain.
"He "only ask that we abide.

You'll never have too much to bear
Though you hurt throughout your soul.
That's "His" promise that we share.
"He "again will make us whole.

"DAY BY DAY "

"Lord, please clear the anger from my heart,
Let forgiveness be my rule.
I'll love my neighbor and myself
And never, never will be cruel."

"God will, be there by my side,
No matter what may come my way.
He gives me insight to "His" plan,
Through the shadows of my day."

"I care what's right or wrong
But sometimes it's hard to choose.
Guide me Lord, through thick and thin.
I pray "Your "love I'll never lose."

"I Praise You Lord for every day.
Your precious blood You shed for me.
Plant my feet on solid ground
And let "Your" Spirit set me free."

"In everything I do or say,
Lord help me choose the proper way.
On You my burdens I will lay,
To help me make it" DAY BY DAY."

"BIDING TIME "

"Biding Time" is truly an art.
When one has suffered a broken heart.

Patience wear thin, life is hard to endure,
When one feels lost and insecure.

Seek out your virtues, find the new you,
The one snuffed out by your feeling blue.

Waite for contentment, it WILL come your way
Build on your assets, don't waste a day.

"STARTING ANEW"

It isn't easy to start anew
With lifelong habits instilled in you.

You're apt to find that you are confused
Without the props you have always used.

Your health, wealth, honor and pride
And the feeling of security you had inside.

These are gone forever? Think this never!
They can be built back, stronger than ever.

Just pick up the pieces and put them in place.
You have yourself and the world to face.

"DON'T USE OTHERS"

Don't use others to get your way.
By telling them what to do or say.

It may seem to you like you have won
And no one knows what you have done.

God knows about our every act
And He knows if it is false or fact.

Ask for forgiveness, of your woes,
And apologize to your foes.

"SOMEONE HELP ME PLEASE!

"I need someone to help me, please!
Help me change my troubled life to ease".

Surely there is someone who will really care,
To know my sorrows and will their love share.

Why did God put me on this place
called Earth?
I'm such a lonely one and feel no self-worth.

Then someone seemed to be right
there by my side.
He said, "Come with me and by my rules
abide."

"There is someone who cares,
someone very near
That can help you face this life without fear.

"Thank you for this one of whom you speak."
"I'll treat them with love and be so ever meek."

My heart began to lighten as I began to see.
The "Someone", God was speaking of was
"ME."

"IT WAS WORTH IT"

I told the Lord that I could bear my life
no longer.
Then He took my hand and gently guided me.
Each new sorrow that was mine just made me
stronger.
Once He put me where He wanted me to be.

He healed my heart, calmed my fears and
made me humble.
He enabled me to have more love
within my heart.
Without this love He knew that I would surely
stumble.
Before the healing of my life could ever start.

Through the shadows of my past, I again found
my faith.
He gave me strength and endurance for a
new start
And encouragement to follow in His path.
So the sadness of my past could now depart.

It was worth it, yes it was worth it.
Even though sometimes I suffered pain.
He allowed it, yes He allowed it'
So the insight of His love I could obtain.

"TRIBUTE TO THE HOBO"

There is much to be said
Of the lowly hobo.
And it may not all be
A tall tale of woe.
His main concern is that
He will be fed
And have a place at night
To lay his head.

From East coast to West
He is free to roam.
He goes where he pleases
The world is his home.
There is no time clock
For him to punch.
And he never goes to a boring
Business lunch.

He has no alimony or taxes to pay.
Not too bad when you
See it that way!

"THE RULE Of THUMB FOR THE INDEX FINGER"

The "index finger", the one usually used
In pointing at someone who is being accused,

Can cause your integrity to be jeopardized.
Even your character can be criticized.

Before that finger is pointed in making attack,
Be sure what you think you know is fact.

There is a good rule to follow when you feel temptation.
This may save you and your foe humiliation.

"The Rule Of Thumb", as it is so defined.
Has two qualities which are great when combined.

So take heed! Experience and Common sense.
For the index finger, forever hence.

"THE TRUNK"

I was laden with undue burdens
Laying heavy on my heart.
I went to the alter and prayed,
"God please let them depart."

But when I arose from praying,
I did not feel anew.
"Yes" I had picked those burdens up
And took them to my pew.

So I still had hate and anger
And all that sordid junk.
This time I put them in writing
And packed them in my trunk.

I hauled that trunk back to the alter,
It was packed clear full.
It was heavy and took all of my strength
Just to tug and pull.

"I can't handle them, I need "Your "tact.
I give them all to "Thee."
This time forever "Lord, "no hauling back."
"Please set my spirit free."

"I was sincere, the Lord knew this well
As I knelt there to pray.
"So He took my trunk of peril
And whisked it right away."

"LEFT BEHIND"

We are those left behind
After a series of life ravishing storms.
We are remnants of families
With tear stained hearts and souls
That are tattered and torn.

We must wipe our tears
And mend each shattered thread.
We must make new memories.
And not ask "why",
Nor fear what lies ahead.

Yes "we" are left behind.
We are families'
We are friends.
We are loved ones.
With Christ our common bond.

We must move on.

"FRIENDSHIP"

There is nothing in this life more valuable than
a true friend.
However, to have a true friend,
you have to be one.

Choose your friends carefully!

Some people, looking for a friend are merely
looking for someone to use and make
themselves look good.

Look in the mirror.

This is the one you have to please.
The one you have to trust.

Proceed with caution!

"THE BIBLE WAS RIGHT"

Psalms 34 -18 "The Lord is close to the broken
hearted and saves those who are "Crushed in
Spirit." The Living bible

My spirits were no longer down.
Pease from God came in and turned
my life around.
I resolved the details that were profound
Then my daughter and I moved to another
town.

I got re-acquainted with Joe,
from my hometown.
A good Christian man, his integrity was sound.
We merged our families, with seven
children around.
And a kind hearted mother in law, so endowed

From Joe I gained something
unexplainably sound.
Twenty five Wonderful, Wonderful
Years we found
However, "Wonderful Dreams"
can be unwound.
A second son of mine and his family all
drowned.

Then only five months later, Joe's life ended
so profound.
"This is too much! Help me understand."

I reached out to God and He led me to peace unfound.
"Thank You Lord, I now have my feet on solid ground."

Alone again; However, I have many fond memories around.
I learned that only through God, true peace can be found.
I want others to know this, if their life has been unsound.
If they turn to the Lord for guidance, they too can be calmed.

By: Joyce Martin

"BIDING TIME"

"BIDING TIME" is truly art,
When one has suffered a broken heart.

Patience wear thin, life is hard to endure
When one feels lost and insecure.

Seek out your virtues, find the new YOU,
The one snuffed out by your feeling blue.

Wait for contentment, it will come your way.
Build on your assets, don't waste a day.

"NOT KIND"

Life hasn't always been kind to me.
But for every peril there has been
A blessing twice fold.

The answers haven't always been easy,
But for every doubt there has been
An answer of gold.

It was a rocky road I traveled alone.
But now every day
Is a memory to hold.

"I know time and again I fall short of your way,
But please God, continue to guide me each day."

"JOYCE'S GARDEN"

Standing so tall, so bold, so pink,
The Gerber Daisy just has to think
"So many siblings to watch over from dusk
to dawn."
This is the duty of the first born," YVONNE".

Roses of yellow, so fresh and so bright,
Lovely to see at the very first light.
The truth we now know that yellow was the one,
The only color that could be seen by" JIM",
the first son.

Then came pretty roses of red, the sign of
another son.
Little could we know his life would have
just begun.
When all of a sudden he sailed off to the west,
At age 14, we laid "KENNEY" to rest.

Yellow carnations make statements of
their own.
And their spicy scent allows them to
stand alone.
But to any arrangement, even in yellow, they
can add fire.
This has often been "JANICE'S" job, perhaps
her desire.

A purple Iris, a flower so regal and of
such beauty,

*Always alert (perhaps nosey), but always
on duty.
Remembering things from when she was just a
small child.
"BRENDA" is rambunctious, but never, well
hardly ever, wild.*

*Baby's breath tucked in all around
For the many grandchildren,
"JOYCE" has found.
She has nurtured her garden
with help from above,
And Joyce's Garden will continue to bud from
her LOVE.*

*By: Brenda Simmons, Daughter of;
Joyce Martin*

"TIME"

I want to thank my
Friend for the TIME ,
So freely given to me and my family
When we were in despair.

For the companionship, friendship
And the compliments so TIMELY given.'
We cried, laughed, played, prayed,
Danced and traveled,

With confidence and doubts.
"Time does not wait for anyone."
Yet, TIME is all
That actually counts.

"A LIFE IS A LIFE"

A life is a life is a life on earth,
Till God says otherwise.

To someone as kind and gentle as Wayne
It's hard to say our goodbyes.

Holding firm to his faith,
He passed this on to his heirs.

He never spoke an unkind word.
And would always offer love and prayers.

"PASS IT ON"

Don't blame others for your woes.
We have all been vandeled.
However we will be judged,
On how the events were handled.
To simply test our faith,
Those woes may have been a seed,
Planted by our Savior
To see if we take heed.

What are looked upon as barriers,
May be a bridge in fact
To help us over troubles
And keep our souls intact.
We can separate ourselves
From the life we want to leave.
Spiritual health can thrive
And a new life we can weave.
Then when peace has come
And all fears are gone,
Thank the Lord,
And "PASS IT ON".

"MEMORIES"

What a treasure of memories are
mine to keep.
I can draw on this resource
any time I seek.

This can change my mood from a bed of gloom
To thoughts of beauty like a rose in bloom.

It's a shame these fond memories can't be
passed around.
Among those who don't know what joy can be
found,

By thanking the Lord for the good in each day
And making the most of what comes their way.

God carries my burdens from days in my past,
And gives me memories from which sorrow
has been cast.

"LOOKING BACK"

When you look on life
And only trouble see.
Ask yourself this question,
"Does the trouble lie in me?"

Did you overlook happiness?
Not let it penetrate your mind?
It may have been right before you
If you had only taken time.

Take a second look,
Look at all the joys.
Remember your children
As little girls and boys.

Remember the love you had
And gave with all your might.
Look back again, a different picture
May come to light.

"IN GODS TIME"

Peace, Love, Happiness and Calm.
All will happen
"In God's Time".

Who, Why, When and Where?
All will be answered
"In God's Time".

Time to Pray, Question and Teach,
We will be given,
"In God's Time".

A time to Sing, Play and Smile
We will receive.
"In God's Time."

Love, Comfort and Peace,
Will be our reward,
"IN GOD'S TIME."

CPSIA information can be obtained
at www.ICGtesting.com
Printed in the USA
FSOW02n0348180216
17059FS

9 781498 456111